Patrons arriving for the opera during the 1950s. The climbers on the house are (left to right) *Wisteria sinensis*, *W. sinensis* 'Alba' and *Akebia quinata*.

A plan of the garden appears on page 76.

GLYNDEBOURNE

A Garden for All Seasons

David Wheeler

With drawings by Simon Dorrell

THE
BRYANSGROUND
PRESS

First published in 2000
by The Bryansground Press
Bryan's Ground
Stapleton (Nr Presteigne)
Herefordshire LD8 2LP

ISBN 0-9538230-0-8

Typeset in Van Dijck
Printed and bound in Great Britain by Smith Settle, Otley, Yorkshire

. . . Here murmurs the stream, here sports the breeze,
Which refreshes the heart with its sweet whispers.
Here flowers smile and the grass is cool;
Here everything invites to the pleasures of love.
Come, my dearest, and amid these sheltered trees
I will wreathe thy brow with roses.

Susanna in *The Marriage of Figaro*. Act IV, Scene Ten

CONTENTS

INTRODUCTION

The graciousness of civilisation here surely touches
a peak, where the arts of music, architecture, and
gardening combine for the delight of man.
Vita Sackville-West, 1952

Although Glyndebourne Festival Opera had earned itself a place on the world's stage long before I was born, I feel a curious link to its earliest days. As a young man in 1973 — when the best stalls seat cost all of £8 — I was taken to see *Figaro* (coincidentally, a new production of Glyndebourne's first staged event) by a friend who had been taken by his mother to the opening season in 1934 (best seats £2!). Under my friend's generous stewardship I became a regular visitor, and in addition to the music, the conviviality of the place, the fine food and drink, I became absorbed by the garden, noticing small changes on each return visit. That initial string of yearly encounters with Glyndebourne ended with my friend's death in 1984, and I only became a routine visitor again during the last days of the old theatre, in 1992.

Like many Glyndebourne addicts, I had to do without my fix while the new opera house was being built in 1993 — although the Company kept its flag flying in London that summer with semi-staged performances at the Royal Festival Hall. Like a returning swallow (but dressed as a penguin) I made the journey to the Sussex Downs once more in the summer of 1994, shortly after the new theatre opened. Along with everyone else I was impatient to experience the modernist auditorium designed by Michael Hopkins & Partners, curious to know how old and new buildings had been stitched together, and anxious to see what remained of the treasured, timeworn garden.

Glyndebourne is a private domain, a place for family and friends, generously shared with singers and musicians, back-stage staff, maintenance crew, and a three-month invasion of day-long, ticket-holding summer migrants. The

Glyndebourne seen from its parkland, September 1999

garden is an 'extra', something you are given for the afternoon and evening, and, warts and all, it has burrowed its way into the hearts of the thousands of us who are fortunate enough to go there each season. Glyndebourne without its fragrant borders and shady walks is as unimaginable as Glyndebourne without its Christies, without its opera.

This book has been arranged in such a way as to offer glimpses of each part of the garden, concentrating on just some of the hundreds of plants grown there. Few if any are prominently labelled. This may be frustrating for green-fingered visitors anxious to learn the name of something which catches their eye, but tagging of every clump and bough could only result in a spoilation of aesthetic values. Nor can a book of these modest dimensions list (or attempt to list) every plant to be found in Glyndebourne's twelve cultivated acres. However, to discover the name of a particular plant, it is possible to leave a note for the Head Gardener, giving a brief description and a clue as to where the enigma grows.

Acknowledgements

As ever, foremost thanks to Liz Robinson and Simon Dorrell. I should like to thank the Christie family heartily for their help and inspiration, and for allowing me to tramp through their private world at very odd hours. Thanks are also due to Glyndebourne's shop and gallery manager Ros Roscoe (who sowed the seed), archivist Julia Aries, press officer Joanna Townsend, former Head of Press Helen O'Neill, photographer Mike Hoban and, of course, Glyndebourne's gardeners Chris, Ron, Steve and Kevin. I am grateful also to Christopher Lloyd, OBE, and Mary Keen, whose imprints are on the garden and who, after reading the typescript, made valuable suggestions.

I should also like to thank those members of the Glyndebourne company who gave me their own garden reminiscences, even though most were unfit to print!

For her typographical and layout skills and for overseeing the production of this book, thanks also to Alison Tristram.

Many friends of Glyndebourne have generously contributed money, plants, seats and artefacts to the new gardens, and a list of these patrons and donors was given on page 138 of the 1994 Festival Programme, and in successive programmes.

A Glyndebourne pug on the plinth carrying John Christie's bust

THE GARDEN'S HISTORY

Glyndebourne, 1783

An account book for 1722, at the dawning of a Golden Age for opera in Europe — but long before this Sussex house reverberated to the sound of the human voice lifted in song — shows that there were five labourers then working in the garden at Glyndebourne. A year later the estate employed nine men, including part-timers, some of whom occasionally worked in the garden; but 1723 seems to have been a year of unrest, for a record of 2nd November states that all workmen ('except for David') were dismissed. (Unrest was also notable in the operatic world: 1723 was the year Handel threatened to throw his leading soprano, Francesca Cuzzoni, out of a window if she continued her troublesome ways.) Between April and June of 1724, the year Handel's *Giulio Cesare* was first seen and heard at London's Haymarket Theatre and the score of *Rodelinda* (first performed in 1725) was drying on the page, a terrace wall along Glyndebourne's south front was built, and in September six men were employed to level the garden.

Glyndebourne's history, like that of many another old English estate, wanders sinuously back in time, weaving its path through several families and over many generations, each of which has left its signature on the buildings and the land.

In his entertaining and minutely detailed history of Glyndebourne, Spike Hughes tells us that opera houses have 'always been built on the sites either of demolished churches (particularly in Catholic countries) or of earlier theatres that have been burnt down . . . [but] . . . never, so far as anybody [is] aware, . . . in the garden of an English gentleman's country house . . .' In antiquity, however, the church did play a small role in Glyndebourne's existence. Mr Hughes explains:

> Until the Reformation the Archbishops of Canterbury owned extensive property in the neighbourhood of Lewes, and there are still to be found in Sussex parishes known as 'Peculiars' whose churches, like those of the two villages closest to Glyndebourne, Ringmer and Glynde, for instance, while geographically in the diocese of Chichester, were in fact in the peculiar jurisdiction of the See of Canterbury . . .
>
> The Manor of Malling [a present-day parish of Lewes] is mentioned in Domesday; the Manor of Glynde is not, but it seems to have been established as part of the Manor of Malling not long after William the Conqueror's survey and in due course to have been conveyed by the Archbishop by sub-infeudation to a family who took their name from the village and were known as de Glynde.

Sometime around 1300 the manor passed by marriage into the Walley family, and in the last decade of the fifteenth century a Walley heiress married Nicholas Morley, member of 'an ancient and respectable family which had its original seat at Morley in Lancashire.' A century further on, one Mary Morley married John Hay of Herstmonceux in Sussex, and it is thought that the small house known as Glynde Bourne (usually given as two words until the nineteenth century) served as part of her marriage dowry in 1589. John and Mary Hay had five children, and their eldest son, Herbert (an orphan by the age of 14), bought the Glyndebourne estate in 1618.

In 1650 Sarah Hay, one of Herbert's thirteen children, married Sir John Langham of Cottesbrooke (a house in Northamptonshire whose garden was the subject of a book published in the 1980s). The Christies (originally

Glyndebourne, 1868

Christin,* from Switzerland) came to Glyndebourne after the marriage between Daniel Béat Christin and Sarah Hay's descendant Elizabeth Langham: it was their son, Langham Christie, born in 1789, who was bequeathed the estate under the terms of the wills of the last two Hay sisters.

Still there is no evidence that any formal garden existed, yet by 1846 trees had been planted by the second pond, and the lawns which 'extended for thirty chains [some 650 yards] swept across the ha-ha and field beyond.'

On Langham Christie's death at the age of 72 in 1861, Glyndebourne passed to his son William Langham Christie (MP for Lewes from 1874 to 1885), who in 1855 had married Agnes Hamilton Clevland of Tapeley Park in Devon, a house which remains in the Christie family to this day. Agnes brought money as well as property into the Christie family, allowing an increase of the Glyndebourne estate to 10,000 acres.

* The family name Christin was 'Anglicised' when Daniel joined the East India Company.

Glyndebourne, 1878

John Christie, born at Tapeley Park in 1882, founder of Glyndebourne Festival Opera in 1934, was the grandson of William and Agnes; his father Augustus Christie married Lady Rosamond Alicia Wallop (a name that lives on in Glyndebourne's Over, Middle and Nether Wallop restaurants), a daughter of the fifth Earl of Portsmouth.

After leaving Cambridge John Christie became a science master at Eton. He had already developed a taste for Wagner's music and in 1904 had travelled to Bayreuth to indulge his new passion. In 1922, a bachelor of 40, he settled permanently at Glyndebourne and there devoted himself to the estate and to a string of exciting projects, filling the house with friends whom he entertained with outdoor games, shooting parties, and music. The garden must have been the setting for many happy tea-parties and leisurely saunters.

Langham Christie had built a Fives Court at the east end of the house in the 1850s, and a conservatory was later added to its front wall; both were demolished in the early 1920s to make way for the Organ Room where, more

Top: Site of the original opera house in the Walled Garden
Above: The newly-built opera house, 1934

than a decade before the staging of Glyndebourne's first opera, vocal and instrumental concerts were given, and the Lewes Music Festival occasionally used the room for rehearsals. (A programme for concerts given in September 1921 — before completion of the great organ — requests that the audience be quiet during the performance, but invites them 'to talk and shuffle as much as they wish between the pieces'.)

Recitals and chamber concerts in the Organ Room soon gave way to the presentation of scenes from opera, with John Christie himself taking a leading role in one instance. And in 1930, when the soprano Dorothy Gibson was unavailable for a planned extract from Mozart's *Die Entführung*, the role of Blonde was taken by Audrey Mildmay, a young member of the Carl Rosa Company.

Within six months of their meeting, Audrey Mildmay (also from a Herstmonceux family) and the affable and hugely gregarious John Christie were married. After their honeymoon John Christie began to plan an extension to the Organ Room, but over dinner one night Audrey cautioned that this might not be the best way forward: 'If you're going to spend all that money, John, for God's sake do the thing properly.' Her words proved the catalyst, and construction of a complete new theatre began in 1931. With the exterior appearance of a Sussex barn, it occupied ground in the Walled Garden, immediately behind the Organ Room, and seated 311 people. As John Jolliffe says, 'Not since Count Esterházy built his opera house for Haydn at Esterháza had there been such a magnificent example of private musical enterprise.' The curtain rose on 28th May 1934. Appropriately, the opera was Mozart's *Marriage of Figaro*, with its convoluted last act set in a garden; Audrey Mildmay sang the role of Susanna.

The prospectus for that first season advertised the outdoor attractions:

The Opera House is surrounded with beautiful lawns and gardens which will be at the disposal of the public. Within a quarter-of-a-mile's stroll of the house is a chain of woodland pools following the course of a Downland stream, leading to coppices carpeted with wild flowers. The grounds are encircled by gracious hills and in whichever direction one looks the eye is met by views of unspoiled natural loveliness.

Members of the audience in the garden during the first season, 1934

By this time the gardens at Glyndebourne were under the steady and hardworking hands of Frank Harvey; he had first worked there in the Twenties, and was now responsible for laying out parts of the garden which can still be seen today. His appointment was made by John Christie (who didn't want a 'Victorian gardener') after the briefest of interviews and on the grounds that he could grow grapes, and peas, and celery. (An earlier attempt had been made at Glyndebourne to grow grapes, at some time during the 1700s, and the miserable outcome of that venture resulted in an area opposite the front drive becoming known as The Vinegars.) Harvey remained as Head Gardener until 1960, and was mentioned in each season's Festival programme. He shared with his employer a fondness for ordinary plants: a clump of buttercups in a border would often be left, rather than dug out.

Setting up a picnic by the Pond, 1958

The vogue for garden picnics at Glyndebourne has grown up since the end of the Second World War. In the Thirties it was announced that patrons might 'bring their own refreshments and consume them in the Dining Hall, and in this case may, if they wish, be waited on by their own servants'. There may be few servants among the al fresco crowd today, but there is much competition in the matter of table decoration, and regrettably the elaborate candelabra on the lawns can sometimes far outnumber those to be seen on any stage set representing some eighteenth-century Viennese salon.

During the autumn months of 1952 the theatre was enlarged, encroaching further on the walled garden: for the 1953 season there were to be 718 seats. But this was a sad year. The death of Audrey Mildmay, at just 52, was announced a week before the season opened; John Christie himself died in 1962. His son George took over the helm with his wife Mary, whom he married in 1958, and Glyndebourne entered a new era, one that was to astound the opera-going world.

George and Mary Christie 'wear the opera house as a natural, permanent garment', wrote Spike Hughes in 1965. Mary's friendship with Christopher Lloyd — acting in the capacity of 'adviser and recommender' — has brought many new ideas to the garden, but their association has also seen the sorry loss of many of the estate's grand trees, first in the late 1970s through Dutch elm disease and then in that famous violent storm of October 1987 which wrought havoc across a wide swathe of south-eastern England. High winds caused hundred-year-old beech trees to crash to the ground, and uprooted mature limes. Head Gardener Chris Hughes, then newly on the payroll, remembers the chaos and devastation, and the vast amount of time and energy needed to clear away the debris. Some of the smaller limbs torn from willows around the pond were later planted beside the water, and have themselves since grown into trees.

However, the biggest change of 1987 was man's work, rather than an Act of God, though it too involved dynamic alterations of a horticultural nature. Sir George (knighted in 1984 for his services to opera) and Lady Christie announced that the existing theatre was to be demolished, and that a replacement — with a larger auditorium (1250 seats), better back-stage and rehearsal facilities and the very latest in technical contrivances — would rise from the rubble, with the loss of only one opera season. It seemed an impossible challenge, but £34m were privately raised, and the architects Michael Hopkins & Partners came up trumps.

House and Theatre from the garden

It was clear that in the train of this upheaval, parts of the garden would require to be remodelled and entirely new spaces designed and planted, so professional help was sought. Nick Lawrence's Landscape Management firm worked in tandem with Mary Keen, a consultant designer well used to working on a country-house scale. It was their daunting task, in collaboration with the family and the team of gardeners, to ensure that everything looked right on the opening night in May 1994. 'Luckily,' writes Mary Keen, opera-goers 'were not allowed to see the well-loved places turned to a sea of mud, where the giant crane held sway.' By a hair's breadth the deadline was met, though of course it was a season or two before some of the newer areas had established themselves.

On 31st December 1999, on the occasion of his sixty-fifth birthday at a millennium party on the Glyndebourne stage for friends and staff, Sir George officially handed over control of the opera company to his second son. With Augustus Christie, his wife Imogen and their young children, yet another era begins. Who can say how the garden will change? One thing is certain: it *will* change — for, as the English novelist H. E. Bates once pronounced, 'a garden that is finished is a garden that is dead.'

HOW THE GARDEN GROWS

Glyndebourne means different things to different people, but whatever it means tends to involve the garden. Even those who work there — on the stage, in the pit, behind the scenes in different capacities, or in the grounds doing a countless variety of jobs — cannot ignore it, whether it is as no more than a space to pass through on the way from one chore to the next, or as an outdoor staff-room where off-duty moments are shared with friends and colleagues. For many opera-goers (and for critics, too, perhaps), Glyndebourne is the high point of their musical year — offering the chance to spend an afternoon and evening in the grounds of a country house set in some of England's most beautiful downland.

At once a visitor notices the 'open' arrangement of the garden. There are very few secret hideaways, no labyrinth of intricate yew-hedged enclosures where small groups of people can isolate themselves from their fellows. It's as if it had been designed for one big, open-air party. But it was not planned as an entity. Like many old gardens, it has evolved over the years — several hundred years in this case — adapting always to changes in weather, fortune and purpose. But its unfettered layout suits its present role well, and indeed in some ways reflects the decision taken by a gregarious family, some sixty years ago, to spend much of its time in the company of other people.

The Wild Garden Border. Purple-leaved amaranthus seedlings among poppies,
Crocosmia 'Lucifer' and a spray of yellow-flowered *Thalictrum flavum*

Lady Christie once wrote that the Glyndebourne gardens already had a great
reputation in 1958, when she married into the Christie family. 'Much of this
was attributable to the way Mr Frank Harvey, Head Gardener for countless
years, had helped to lay them out in the early 1930s and developed and cared
for them so assiduously until 1959/60.'

Mary Christie says the gardens 'went through quite a bad patch' in the early
Sixties; but, recognising their inherent quality, she considered it her job 'to
try and guarantee that the pedigree shows well — like a dog at Crufts.' (The
canine metaphor reflects the whole family's devotion to pugs.) It is a job well
done, by dint of Mary Christie's ability to work easily with other people, to
listen to professionals, and to go along with what's shown to be best.
Nevertheless, she seems always to instil something of herself into any scheme
under consideration. Her minor battles with Christopher Lloyd — over
colours, in particular — are an example: Mary Christie (sometimes) wins. 'It's
her garden and I never forget that,' says Mr Lloyd.

Christopher Lloyd has held an informal 'watching brief' at Glyndebourne for more than three decades, sometimes reworking an entire section, sometimes injecting a lively detail to relieve an otherwise monotonous patch — like the sauce chef adjusting the seasoning of a finished dish. His own garden, at Great Dixter on the edge of the village of Northiam, some thirty miles east of Glyndebourne, was largely designed by the architect Sir Edwin Lutyens in the early part of the twentieth century and has become well known today for its owner's experiments with new plants, new colours, new colour combinations, and an altogether new way of approaching the craft of garden making. Given Mary Christie's somewhat 'traditional' views, it's not surprising that one or two of Mr Lloyd's ideas should have failed to take hold. But each respects the other, and if little 'refinements' are made when backs are turned, who's to worry? It would be scarcely possible, after all, for a garden of this size, vintage and present-day function to bear the stamp of only one mind.

Head Gardener Chris Hughes (second from right)
with (left to right) Steve, Kevin and Ron. Spring 2000

Chris Hughes has been at Glyndebourne since the late 1980s; appointed Head Gardener at the age of thirty-two in 1988, he now heads a four-man team whose other members are Ron and Steve Brockhurst (father and son) and Kevin Martin, Ron's son-in-law. In addition to the gardens proper, they look after the Plashett Woods above the car park, the car park itself, and all those small parcels of woodsy land seen by visitors arriving via the back road.

All twelve acres of formally appointed gardens are on very chalky soil which makes it impossible to grow acid-loving plants. It is well, therefore, that no one at Glyndebourne hankers after rhododendrons, or great carpets of heather. 'Indeed,' says Christopher Lloyd, 'Mary Christie revels in not being able to grow them.'

The gardening year has no beginning, and it has no end. There is always something to do — sometimes too much. During the opera season the day's work may begin as early as six o'clock, to ensure it is finished before the first visitors arrive — never, it is hoped, before 2.30. The lawn-mowing regime begins in March, soon increasing from a once-a-week chore to a twice-weekly burden. In a woefully wet summer some areas, such as the Ha-ha Lawn, may need three cuts in a seven-day period. The grass is given a granular feed in spring and autumn, and at the end of the season it is gone over with a scarifying attachment, a piece of equipment that takes out the 'thatch' of dead clippings; then a 'slitter' makes six-inch-long gashes into the turf, to improve drainage and allow air to circulate once more among compacted roots. But there is a kindly side to all this harsh-sounding scarifying and slitting: daisies are not entirely frowned upon — as Christopher Lloyd puts it, 'they humanise an expanse of green turf'.

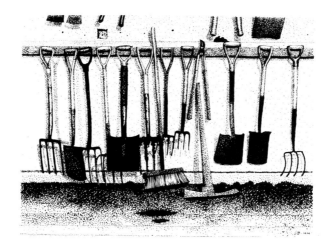

You might imagine an arsenal of heavy-gauge garden machinery to be required for all this work, but there is only one small rotary mower (for tricky corners) and two strimmers, in addition to one ride-on mower, and cutters that can be fixed to the John Deere tractor. Like the hedge-cutters and an indispensable chain-saw, however, these call for day-to-day maintenance as well as a thorough servicing each winter. A formidable battery of hand tools must also be regularly inspected, and replacements ordered for worn-out or broken spades, forks, trowels and all manner of other gear. This vital indoor work is now done in the gardeners' new quarters — a brick building measuring 65 feet by 30. (Their adjacent former quarters, at the far end of the Plashett Building at the foot of the car park, are now occupied by the Archive Department, with extra space to mount yearly exhibits based on Glyndebourne's cornucopian heritage.)

Seeds are mainly sown in spring, although a seed-sowing programme continues throughout the year to provide the hundreds of annuals needed to help furnish borders and fill containers. Cuttings are also taken to provide the annual requirement of something like 350 penstemons and pelargoniums.

Although Glyndebourne is self-sufficient in water, provided by the Estate's own bore-hole on the hill, there is no irrigation system in place. Thirsty borders must sometimes be quenched by hose-pipe, and tender plants growing in the numerous terracotta pots grouped either side of the foyer need almost constant attention with well-filled watering cans throughout the summer.

Groups of tender and half-hardy plants set out for the summer by the foyer

If the spring months are hectic, so too are those of autumn. For two weeks at the end of August and the beginning of September, it's all hands to the hedges.* Then, after hedge-trimming, the great herbaceous cut-back begins, a job calling for several weeks of careful toil with secateurs and garden shears. There are quantities of bulbs to be planted and, in a steady progression around the entire garden, all borders are tidied, forked over, and given a mulch of Glyndebourne's home-made compost — a sustaining and nutritious soil-conditioner composed of miscellaneous garden waste and prodigious amounts of grass clippings. Certain perennials are lifted, divided and replanted on a three-year cycle, to maintain vigour and also to provide new plants for use in other areas, or replace individual worn-out colonies.

'Is it all unrelenting hard work?' I ask Chris. 'Well,' he answers, 'I do get a few moments to reply to visitors who have written to ask the name of a specific plant, or to people who want to donate a tree or a bench to the garden in memory of someone who loved the place.'

'And what else do they write in about?'

'We get a few congratulatory letters, which are always appreciated, and every so often we're asked to look for items of lost property — jewellery, cigarette lighters, that sort of thing, and just occasionally a few things I'd better not mention. Truth to say, when we're working in the borders, we sometimes find rather more than champagne corks!'

---

* Clippings from the yew hedges are collected by a British company and exported to France where they are used to make a drug for the treatment of cancer.

THE TERRACE

Surely everyone, during the course of their afternoon and evening at the opera, makes a *passagiata* along Glyndebourne's Terrace? Two can walk and talk comfortably side-by-side and, if the sun is shining, enjoy the warmth radiating from the brick façade of the house. The planting is bosky and fragrant — bosky, to form a screen between visitors and any family members delighting in a few idle moments on the 'inner', private, terrace; fragrant, to beguile the nose and waft sweet smells from garden to house through open windows.

The show on the Terrace must be kept going all summer long: there must be flowers to greet the earliest visitors in May, and to bid farewell to the last to leave, at the end of August. In fruitful years there will also be much to enjoy during the pre-tour performances scheduled for autumn.

It's a leisurely hundred paces from the Organ Room to the beginning of the rose-clad pergola at the far end, with shrubs, perennials, and a few annuals and bulbs planted in two grand borders either side of the stone path. The glossy-leaved evergreen magnolia (*M. grandiflora*) growing on the walls of the house bears fat parchment-coloured flowers that expand to the size of breakfast plates. Individually each may last only a few days, but a succession appears over a long spell between the middle of July and October. With scent of pre-eminent importance by the house, it is no surprise to see so many fragrant shrubs and climbers revelling in this southerly aspect. The summer-flowering jasmine (*J. officinale*) scrambling over the Organ Room's great bay windows is no parvenu in English gardens. Commonly called the poet's jasmine, it's thought to have been grown in Britain since the sixteenth century. Given a favoured spot, such as it enjoys here, it will flower as liberally as in its homeland, that vast tract stretching from northern Iran, through the Himalayas and into China, and its dainty white blooms know no modesty when it comes to pushing out the perfume.

A plant that's been with us for almost as long, but of a slightly more tender constitution (and far less commonly seen in British gardens), is *Cestrum parqui*, from Chile, planted at Glyndebourne in the skirts of the tangled jasmine. Related to the humble potato (and to deadly nightshade and the solanum which flails about the Green Room's oriel window), the cestrum, like this garden's much-loved tobacco plants, is a night bird. Other after-dark wafters

The Terrace borders during the 1950s

The Terrace in early May. Flame-coloured *Euphorbia griffithii* 'Dixter'
and seedling columbines (*Aquilegia*)

banded together here include daphne, heliotrope (bedded-out annually), a good-sized bush of honeyed *Euphorbia mellifera*, pineapple-scented *Cytisus battandieri* (a successful grey-leaved immigrant from Morocco) and, most recently planted, a Chinese climbing honeysuckle, *Lonicera similis* var. *delavayi*. Also from far afield — New Zealand — but flowering earlier in the year is *Pittosporum tenuifolium*, dear to florists in their constant search for year-round greenery to bulk up bouquets. This distinctive evergreen has tiny yet highly-charged purply-brown flowers in spring. The two specimens now on the Terrace replace a much larger pittosporum which died after a hard winter several years ago.

The two yew 'cubes' mark the dividing point between old planting and new: here — where ancient and modern brush shoulders, so to speak — you must come at dusk to experience a noseful of concentrated perfume, and here, as many of the strongly-scented flowers are truly nocturnal, you should return for one last draught of sweet Sussex air before piling into your car at the end of the evening. This potent cocktail, mixed with the piquancy of cotton-

The Terrace in late June. Tall spikes of yellow verbascum with *Salvia sclarea* var. *turkestanica* and (right) the grey foliage of *Artemisia ludoviciana*

lavender leaves and with equally night-generous tobacco plants, will set you up for a return to the rigours of everyday life.

A motley chorus of perennials animates the Terrace, in a range of colours from pale cream to deepest mahogany red. The borders are not mirror images of each other, yet many plants are represented on both sides. Some, like the blue perennial salvias and a host of penstemons (including 'Alice Hindley', 'Firebird', 'Rich Ruby' and 'Stapleford Gem'), dart from side to side. The cleome, or spider flower (the one with the pink-and-white punk hair-do), is a striking newcomer to the border whose somewhat quieter cousin, in sober magenta, stands a little distance away. The daturas look exotic, their long, drooping flowers seemingly at rest. The species in these borders, *Datura innoxia*, has several common names, including downy thorn apple, Indian apple and, best of all, angel's trumpet. Considering that daturas come from Central America, it's remarkable that those left to overwinter out of doors do sometimes survive the whims of a Glyndebourne winter without coming to harm.

Ilse Bing on the Terrace steps, 1937

Clumps of purple tradescantia look as if they belong in a heated greenhouse, and stiff branching spires of yellow verbascum, mostly self-sown, punctuate the other plants at irregular intervals all the way along. There are tall brick-red macleayas to sway in the summer breeze, giant pale-yellow scabious on wiry six- to eight-foot stems, and lofty delphiniums (one called 'Faust' has an appropriate ring) provide pillars of conservative blue. The open daisies of *Aster × frikartii* 'Mönch', one of the earliest asters to bloom in this country, contribute a much paler blue. Then there are the dahlias, returning now to English gardens after a twenty-year exile imposed by the diktats of 1980s garden chic. Their heads of ultra-confident colour need careful placing, even in such a cosmopolitan gathering as this. 'Gloire van Heemstede' is known as a water-lily dahlia, and its lightweight yellow flowers go on for weeks and weeks atop unbending four-foot stems. 'Debra Ann Craven' is a large-flowered semi-cactus dahlia with deep red flowers, while 'Berwick Wood', classified as a decorative dahlia, has purply-pink petals. The aristocrat of the dahlias in this border, however, and one keenly advocated by connoisseurs of single-theme, all-red flower borders, is 'Bishop

Top left: *Cistus* 'Elma' Top right: *Eupatorium purpureum*
Middle left: *Clematis integrifolia* Middle right: *Hemerocallis fulva*
Bottom left: *Penstemon* 'Firebird' Bottom right: *Heliotropium arborescens* 'Marine'

of Llandaff', whose attractions lie just as much in his garb of bronzy-green summer foliage as in his simple scarlet flowers.

Towards the far (western) end of the Terrace, on the side nearest the house, is the famous stand of Glyndebourne crinums (*Crinum* × *powellii*). Originating from Tapeley Park, the Christie family house in Devon, these bulbs have given faithful service to at least four generations of the family; in Christopher

Looking west along the Terrace, 1939

Looking south-east across the Terrace, 1984

Lloyd's estimation, they have been on the Glyndebourne Terrace, crowded and undisturbed, for the last fifty years. They soldier on, their gigantic bulbs half out of the ground, their slashed and broken leaves having an air of unmade beds about them, but in late summer these slovenly habits are readily forgiven as stems carrying ten or more delicate pale trumpets rise above the mass of ragged foliage. Of perhaps a similar vintage are the yuccas, whose flower spikes of ivory bells appear each summer.

Despite the necessity for so many summer-performing perennials, all is not lost in winter. Shrub roses, buddlejas, a large bush of *Hebe* 'Midsummer Beauty', a vintage *Osmanthus delavayi* and a glad mixture of evergreen climbers on the low wall contribute to a permanent backbone of shape and form.

Behind the bench at the far end of the Terrace grows the climbing hydrangea *H. petiolaris*, a vigorous, self-clinging species whose leaves turn buttery yellow

The Terrace in July. Spires of verbascum with *Inula magnifica*

before they drop in autumn. If you pause at this bench in July you will detect the highly-fragrant flowers of the pink rose 'Louise Odier', growing next to the door in the wall. Opposite, flanking steps down to the Ha-ha Lawn (and growing 'better here than anywhere I have seen it in Britain', says Christopher Lloyd), is a rigid evergreen mantle of *Danaë racemosa*, the Alexandrian laurel, tolerant of deep shade yet happy, if the summer has been long and hot, to deck itself in autumn with a scattering of orangey-red fruits.

But why stop here? On stifling, sun-drenched afternoons visitors are drawn inexorably on through the tunnel-like pergola, festooned with pale blooms. Notes and labels have long since been lost, so that no one at Glyndebourne now knows for certain the names of these roses, but the pergola's scented shade is inviting, and so too is the curved stone seat on its raised dais which terminates the vista.

Argyranthemum 'Pink Australian' and *Helichrysum petiolare*
in the vase beyond the Terrace pergola

THE HA-HA LAWN

With its brick- or stone-faced dry ditch separating garden from parkland, the ha-ha is a cunning seventeenth-century French device for giving a garden the appearance of flowing seamlessly into the countryside beyond. No fence or other visual barrier interrupts the view to open fields, the garden looks much larger than it really is ('Aha!'), and grazing animals are barred from trespass. If built well, it should last forever with no more than basic maintenance. England's first ha-ha, though shorter than the one at Glyndebourne, is thought to be that built at Levens Hall in Cumbria. In Sussex's neighbouring county of Hampshire the naturalist Gilbert White of Selborne* recorded on 24th January 1761 that 'Long the mason finish'd the dry wall of the Haha in the new garden.' The idea quickly spread from one estate to another as landowners came to appreciate its benefits and — when labour and building materials were cheaply procurable — its relatively low cost. The Glyndebourne ha-ha, reset in its present position in 1936, displays fourteen courses of brick which, mortared, give the ideal height (or depth, depending on your viewpoint) of approximately six feet — beyond the capabilities and even the imagination of the most energetic of cows, apart from that which Jumped Over the Moon, of course.

* Gilbert White was a regular visitor to nearby Ringmer, home of his aunt, Rebecca Snooke, and her tortoise, Timothy, famed for his longevity and prone to 'snoozing under the mud in the herbaceous border'; an eventual post-mortem examination discovered Timothy to have been a female.

Enclosed by the ha-ha itself, by the retaining wall of the Terrace and by the two narrow borders running each side from the house out to the fields, the Ha-ha Lawn is an acre of carefully nurtured greensward (sown by former head gardener Frank Harvey before the last war) — probably the world's largest (completely organic) opera foyer, restaurant and al fresco crush bar. For, weather always permitting, it is to the Ha-ha Lawn in front of the house that many people flock to set out their tables for the interval picnic, and it's through this animated throng of elegantly dressed ticket-holders that everyone passes *en route* to or from the auditorium.

Immediately beside the steps down to the Ha-ha Lawn, close to the Organ Room, stands Glyndebourne's venerable mulberry, *Morus nigra*, probably the oldest tree on the estate, considerably reduced in size by the 1987 storm. Mulberries have a 'versatile' sexuality, and in his 1983 book about the garden, written with Anne Scott-James, Christopher Lloyd informs us that this particular specimen bears both male and female flowers (on separate branches), enabling it to yield fruit with fertile pips and thus holding out the pleasing possibility of sapling mulberries cropping up elsewhere in the garden. Shade is at a premium on hot summer days, but visitors should be warned of the consequences of plonking themselves down on the cool grass beneath the mulberry: the ripe fruit has powerful staining properties.

Around the Green Room's oriel window, in the Wigs Border, grow the tangled tendrils of the white potato vine (*Solanum jasminoides* 'Album'). Sadly, its great show of white flowers is without perfume, but as a sop they display themselves ceaselessly, all summer long.

Ceanothus thyrsiflorus var. *repens* in the Blue Border

The Blue Border, replanted in the winter of 1989, acts as a low barrier —
almost literally a *cordon bleu* — between the Courtyard Garden and the Ha-ha
Lawn. Dominated by seven dark green Irish yews, this long narrow border
distils shades of blue and mauve into a haze of co-ordinated colour. As with
all single-colour planting schemes, a touch of something else — in this case,
silver foliage — helps to improve the magic, emphasising the principal
colour and at the same time solving the sometimes tricky conundrum of
combining the pure blues of, for example, love-in-a-mist and *Salvia patens*
with the more widespread pinky-blues of perovskia, ajuga, agapanthus and,
famously, lavender.

Lavender and perovskia, together with common sage and certain buddlejas,
are the perfect plants for such designs as these. Their own silvery grey and
blue livery of foliage and stem allows them to settle snugly and at once into
harmony with the artemisias whose filigreed silver leaves weave their way
throughout the border. *Cerinthe major* 'Purpurascens', a plant fashionably new
to gardens in this country, is ideally suited to this border. Sometimes it's hard
to see where leaf ends and flower begins, so imbued are both with a mysterious

The Blue Border. Left to right: *Delphinium requienii*, *Salvia superba* and *S. interrupta*

thunder-cloud purple. The cerinthe, from starved and dry Mediterranean coastlands, makes itself curiously at home in England's damper soils, and well-grown specimens may reach two feet in height. With little encouragement its knobbly black seeds, the size of a match-head, will work their way into paving cracks and lawn-edges to ensure a scattering of additional plants each year.

Another plant in this border that hails from warmer climes and whose name hardly trips from the tongue is *Ceanothus thyrsiflorus* var. *repens*, a California lilac known as creeping blue blossom. It has pale blue powder-puff flowerheads that last for weeks on end, on a bush which will have made a sizeable mound in only a few years. It is not perhaps a notably long-lived shrub in this country, and seemingly healthy specimens have a way of turning up their toes in winter — in the mysterious and frustrating manner of rosemary — without having given any previous notice. Not like buddleja, a toughy equally at home whether fussed over in a well-tended garden or left to its own devices on a derelict building site.

Catmint (*Nepeta*) is another plant of hardy constitution. To ensure generous yearly production of its matt-green foliage and soft sprays of smoky-blue

Members of the audience by the Blue Border, 1963

flowers you need only cut spent stems to the ground at the end of each season.

The flowers of the irises in this border, 'Bristol Gem' and 'Blue Rhythm', pass early, leaving swords of glaucous foliage to 'mark the spot', before the blue salvias have their day. *Salvia azurea* (the prairie sage from the central United States), as its Latin name suggests, is a good clear sky colour, with just a touch of white in the throats of individual flowers. *Salvia* 'Indigo Spires' is a garden hybrid, found originally at the Huntington Botanical Garden in California. Like many of its kin it may need some winter cosseting if it lacks the protection of a south-facing wall or other sheltered place, but when it's happy it will throw its lax mauvy-tinged flower stems five feet high. Several shades of pure blue are offered by *Salvia patens*, most memorably the light and dark forms named 'Cambridge Blue' and 'Oxford Blue'.

Fragrance lingers here, too — fragrance of leaf. The whiff of sage is known to everyone, but the fruity, aromatic leaves of salvia (some of them with a true blackcurrant scent), of the spreading juniper by the steps, and of lavender and perovskia, all contribute to a mixture of smells released only by touch.

If you cross the Lawn below it, you will see that the retaining wall of the Terrace is draped with catmint and valerian, enlivened here and there with the bright purply-magenta flowers of Bowles's perennial wallflower, the airy wands of pink-flowered toadflax (*Linaria*) 'Canon Went', and a pleasant mottling of variegated periwinkle (*Vinca*). The steps up to the Terrace opposite the Organ Room are sprinkled with a little pinky-white daisy (*Erigeron karvinskianus*) that positively flourishes between bricks and in masonry cracks, and the steps themselves are flanked by the bold flowering grasses *Cortaderia selloana* 'Gold Edge' and feathery *Stipa calamagrostis*.

The flower and shrub border on the far (western) side of the Ha-ha Lawn is a shadier affair than the one wherein the blue plants dwell; here, the afternoon shadows cast by high trees in the adjacent Wild Garden give scope for another kind of gardening, opportunity to grow a quite different group of plants from those happy to have their heads in the sun all day long.

By the steps to the Terrace there's a good head-high staphylea, or bladder nut, whose panicles of creamy-white flowers show up well in the afternoon shade. But shade, remember, doesn't necessarily betoken kindly moisture: neighbouring trees and hedges draw heavily on ground-water supplies and overhead branches can act as an umbrella, diverting rain away from root-runs

Members of the audience in recent years before the evening performance
and during the dinner interval

Solanum jasminoides 'Album' around the Green Room's oriel window

beneath. However, it's also a fallacy to assume that shade-tolerant plants are necessarily fervent moisture-lovers. I'm thinking for a moment of lush-leaved hostas — true, they will relish any water available, but their more urgent requirement is for some protection from the sun to guard their foliage against scorch.

Wrestling under the name 'Big Daddy', and looking good enough to eat (but don't try), is a hosta grown for its handsomely puckered glaucous leaves and its cool-looking white flower-spikes in early summer. Like many hosta cultivars let loose on the world in recent years, 'Big Daddy' comes from Paul Aden, the record-breaking hosta breeder in Baldwin, New York. Paul Aden also has a reputation for raising a multitude of plants with colour variegations, but he's not responsible for the variegated elder which (like the cut-leafed elder also growing on this side of the Lawn) needs shade to protect it from the dire effects of sunburn. *Sambucus nigra* 'Marginata', to allow the variegated elder its full and proper name, was given an Award of Merit as long ago as 1892, just four years after the Royal Horticultural Society introduced this classification of plant honour.

With its rodgersias, shuttlecock ferns, tall macleayas, the lovely late-flowering *villosa* hydrangea (a form of *H. aspera*) and clumps of Solomon's seal, this border is in perfect harmony with the woodland to be found behind the tall yew hedge. I notice, too, that a holm oak (*Quercus ilex*) has seeded itself into this border: given its potential height and spread of eighty feet or more, a decision about its future will soon have to be taken. And it's good to see such healthy-looking bushes of the Mexican orange blossom (*Choisya ternata*) hereabouts. Pinching their glossy green leaves will release a strongly aromatic and long-lasting scent. I once used a choisya leaf as a bookmark and the desiccated remains, when I came across it again several years later, still held its distinctive smell, immediately transporting me back to the all-but-forgotten summer afternoon on which I once lost myself in the book.

In the Wild Garden Border, south from the opening in the yew hedge, there is some brave and blazing colour-work in hand. In summer you will now find, among firm favourites like 'Johnson's Blue' geranium, good old *Alchemilla mollis* and the 'Six Hills Giant' form of catmint, the red dressing-gown tassels of *Amaranthus* 'Red Cathedral', *Salvia* 'Lady in Red' and the flaming, crimson-scarlet oriental poppy, 'Beauty of Livermere'. To further spark the proceedings there's *Crocosmia* 'Lucifer' with its countless flame-red flowers over a thicket of sword-like leaves, fluffy yellow meadow rue (*Thalictrum flavum*), and Spanish broom (*Spartium junceum*), which gives profusely of its wonderfully fragrant, bright-yellow pea-like flowers far into autumn.

THE WILD GARDEN

To one side of the main proceedings, west of the Ha-ha Lawn and behind the yew hedge planted by John Christie and Frank Harvey before the last war, lies the Wild Garden, Glyndebourne's green lung. Like the string of ponds away to the east, it attracts wildlife of many kinds and is home to an array of birds. The majestic estate trees — holm oak (*Quercus ilex*), the fast-growing Turkey oak (*Q. cerris*), cut-leafed beech (*Fagus sylvatica* 'Aspleniifolia'), hornbeam, birch and limes — crowd together in emulation of natural woodland, cradling the Wendy House, 'play home' to several generations of Christie children. But natural woodland it is not. Careful management of this fragile environment is necessary to secure the months-long succession of wild flowers that spring from the turf as if to mimic the background of a Botticelli painting.

A metal 'umbrella', a climbing-frame for the vigorous 'Kiftsgate' rose, now replaces an ancient lime tree which fell in the Great Storm of 1987. Other casualties were mature chestnut trees, and the holm oaks which had hefty branches torn away; trees around the pond were also uprooted.

As early as January the grassy places begin to sparkle with snowdrops, including many of the double-flowered form of our native *Galanthus nivalis*. Among them, shining like newly-minted gold coins in courageous defiance of the worst of winter's cold, are the winter aconites, each yellow flower emerging from its snug ruff of equally shiny leaves. These are followed in

Top: Mown paths through the Wild Garden in May
Above: The Wendy House

February by a haze of lilac-blue crocuses (*C. tommasinianus*), a dynamic and inexpensive little corm for naturalising rough ground. Then come lapis-lazuli-blue scillas that increase rapidly each year, jonquils (*Narcissus jonquilla*), and the spirited, short-stemmed daffodil 'Rip van Winkle', with flowerheads of ragged petals like miniature sunbursts. Bluebells and cowslips follow at that magical moment in early May when delicate leaves unfurling on branches high above begin to filter the sunlight into dappled patches below. In June comes the treat: the orchids, our native bee orchid (*Orchis apifera*) and the pyramidal (*O. pyramidalis*), both of them contented dwellers on this chalky Sussex soil.

As summer approaches, the foliage of early bulbs dies down and the taller perennials flowering in their wake cover their tracks. Overnight, it seems, a froth of white cow parsley (*Anthriscus sylvestris*) emerges, quickly becoming speckled with ox-eye daisies, pale blue cranesbill geraniums and the intensely blue flowers of wild chicory, fluting away on three-foot-high stems. Throughout the summer months the gardeners mow a network of sinuous paths through all this coloured hay. By the end of the opera season, as August tails off and the last flowers are fading — before the grass begins to look like a field of ripe corn — all the wild plants will have had a chance to set and disperse their seeds. Only then is the whole of the Wild Garden scythed, in readiness for the following year's repeat performance.

THE COURTYARD GARDEN

The Courtyard Garden takes its name from the small enclosed area situated behind south-facing double doors between the Green Room and the Rehearsal Stage, below the two Glyndebourne flagpoles. The Courtyard café, unseen by the public, is for members of the company, providing them with food and drink throughout long working days before, during and after the official opera season. Within its cloisters the latest gossip is exchanged, embroidered — and (who knows?) quite possibly invented. Stage and maintenance crews, chorus, soloists and orchestral players alike share the convivial facilities. The long lawn which serves as the Courtyard's overspill on warm days when no visitors are around can hum with the social and professional off-duty chatter of as many as two hundred people.

On the August morning of the 1999 total eclipse of the sun, a day of disappointingly cloudy skies over most other parts of Britain, I was fortunate enough to join this gathering to watch the heavenly spectacle in the fine, clear skies of Sussex. As time ticked towards the moment of optimum blackout (about 98 per cent hereabouts), the crowd fell silent; there were no cheers, no distracting shouts, just a great respect for the marvel being enacted thousands of miles up in the sky. One of the world's leading theatrical ensembles was being momentarily upstaged, and knew it.

Cotinus coggygria 'Royal Purple' in the Crescent Border with foxy seedheads of *Dictamnus albus*

With the growing darkness of mid morning the air temperature dropped. Swifts and swallows began to swirl about the buildings as they do at dusk, and the famous Glyndebourne bats put in a brief appearance; someone said the water-lily flowers on the pond were beginning to close. Mary Christie and I rushed to the Urn Garden, where close inspection revealed a subdued yet striking enhancement of individual flower colours — particularly blues and winey purples. It seemed as if garden had become theatre, and the house lights were going down. An amber glow fell over the scene, yet shadows remained strong and firmly in place.

In near faultless paradox, the eclipse also provided an illuminating lesson in garden design. For a few minutes in the midday gloaming the pale flowers in the White Border shone radiantly, while the colour of those opposite, in the Blue Border, seen from the distance of twenty yards or so, drained away to a feeble tint all but lost amid the dull tones of their own foliage. Lesson: if you're planting in shade and want colour to be noticed, use white and pale shades. Of course, almost any basic gardening book will tell you this, but it was interesting to see the principle demonstrated in such inimitable circumstances.

Top: Stems of *Rubus cockburnianus* in winter
Above: Autumn leaves of *Cotinus coggygria* 'Royal Purple'

A member of the orchestra playing croquet during the interval, 1958

The White Border is just one of two strictly (well, fairly strictly) colour-controlled flower beds at Glyndebourne. In recent years, under Christopher Lloyd's hand, it has doubled in size and is principally aimed at the post-opera darkness, when it achieves its greatest significance. Many of the same plants to be found elsewhere in the garden — irises, penstemons, dahlias, et cetera — are here represented in their white or cream or pale pink forms, with other plants seen only here, like the giant Scotch thistle, *Onopordum acanthium*, a tap-rooted biennial with stems and armour-plated leaves of ghostly hue. It spends its first year as a flat rosette of felty leaves, busily making the root which will support and fuel its acceleration to a towering monster in its second year. Then, like many a tragic heroine of the operatic stage, it flowers and dies. The thistle has a few prickly partners, but of lesser stature; by late summer, the metallic-blue stems and seedheads of thistle-like eryngiums will have bleached to the colour of straw.

Kindlier in all its parts is the evergreen common myrtle (*Myrtus communis*), planted by the yew opening to the Croquet Lawn. In late summer it produces masses of small creamy white flowers, while its glossy foliage, when crushed, emits a piquancy familiar to travellers in Provence and other parts of the Mediterranean. Although usually susceptible to late frosts in this country, myrtle can make a fine hedge — think of the Court of the Myrtles at the Alhambra, where two rows of it flank the reflecting pool. Northern Europeans can only imagine the pleasure to be enjoyed in clipping such long runs of this aromatic shrub.

The Crescent Border is an elaborate medley of flower and foliage. Dark Burgundy reds and opulent purples, softened here and there with pink and pale yellow — or spiked with a dash of orange — emanate from shrub and herbaceous perennial alike. The dahlia named 'David Howard' has late-season pompom-like flowers of a colour which hovers somewhere between ochre and deep amber, but all summer long its dark bronze-tinged leaves will have graced this mixed planting. Darker still are the leaves of *Cotinus coggygria* 'Foliis Purpureis' (a selected form of the Venetian sumach, or smoke bush) that turn to shades of fiery red in autumn. The sumach's summer foliage chimes well against the flower spikes of *Buddleja davidii* 'Pink Beauty' and the more unusual 'Dartmoor', whose shorter, broader flower panicles are of a deep magenta — a colour surprisingly well suited to its surroundings. *Buddleja × weyeriana* 'Golden Glow' (a hybrid of *Buddleja davidii* and the Chilean *B. globosa*) has round flower heads the size of gulls' eggs. Close inspection reveals shades of lilac mixed in with the yolky yellow. Beloved by August visitors is *Hoheria sexstylosa*, a shrub or small tree of New Zealand origins, belonging to the mallow family. In July it covers itself thickly with white saucer-shaped flowers.

The northern sugar cane (*Sorghum vulgare*) is a recent introduction to this border, rising by late summer to six feet in height from spring-sown seed. Experimental plantings such as this keep the borders fresh, and offer new delights to those visitors who return each year. Another débutante is the California lilac *Ceanothus* 'Autumnal Blue', a good choice since it's considered to be among the hardiest of the currently available hybrids for our climate, and will surely harmonise with the inky late-flowering salvias.

THE URN GARDEN

Measuring just forty yards by fifteen, this yew-enclosed space sits in the overall garden rather as an open jewel box might sit on a bedroom dressing-table. It is colourful at all seasons, subdued yet plush even in winter, with ghostly bleached-out stems of flowering grasses, ruddy seed heads and any bright sealing-wax rose hips not yet plundered by hungry birds.

The urn from which this part of the garden takes its name was given to John Christie in memory of his wife by Mrs Cicely Ingram in 1955. Now planted with an agave, and with the pink-flowered *Geranium endressii* at the foot of its plinth, it stands at a point where two brick paths cross each other. The shorter path runs west-east from the Boat House Lawn to the Croquet Lawn — once Glyndebourne's grass tennis court, more recently, weather permitting, the orchestral players' 'Green Room' on performance days. The long path runs to a gap in the yew hedge which frames a view to lofty trees beside the pond and on to the distant Downs.

In days now long past the Urn Garden was Glyndebourne's Rose Garden, and older visitors still reminisce about the heavily-scented rows of 'Mrs Sinkins' pinks that made a low 'hedge' along the paths. (For a while during the war it was also used as an extra vegetable garden.) The layout today is much the same, but the varied, dense and lush replanting, an exuberant mix of shrubs, shrub roses, tall wand-like grasses and stout, rangy perennials such as

The Urn Garden. Top: the urn planted with *Agave americana*. Above: *Stipa gigantea* in September with *Verbena bonariensis* and the light green foliage of *Bassia scoparia*

Top: Frank Harvey in the Urn Garden tending vegetables during the Second World War
Above: Members of the audience in the Urn Garden when it was planted with roses, 1958

hollyhocks, campanulas, acanthus and hardy salvias, has evolved 'through expediency' since Christopher Lloyd redesigned the borders in graduated colours and shades in the 1970s. Its colourful appearance notwithstanding, the Urn Garden remains, curiously, a quiet place; visitors seem to pass on if others are already there, returning later, perhaps, to linger themselves for a few moments, away from the throng.

The ornamental grass at the 'crossroads', guarding the urn, so to speak, is *Stipa gigantea* (commonly called giant feather grass; and because of the plant's colour when fully ripe at the end of summer, it is also known as golden oats). It comes from the Iberian peninsula, but its bone-hardiness has helped establish it securely in gardens throughout the British Isles. Another grass of summer beauty in the Urn Garden is *Pennisetum villosum* (the feathertop grass), which presents itself as a low wave of airy straw-coloured bottlebrushes that sway with the slightest movement of air. The dominant grass is *Arundo donax* (the giant reed and one of appropriate utility given its setting: reeds for oboes and bassoons are made from the stems of this grass). It produces fifteen-foot-high purply-green 'feathers' by late autumn. All these grasses look their best towards the end of the opera season, when wiry-stemmed *Verbena bonariensis* is flowering and the clusters of tall agapanthus seem to reflect the entire Sussex sky in their open blue globes.

The backbone of the Urn Garden's four rectangular beds is made up of tall shrubs and a few roses. Here, seemingly adrift from its native Mediterranean, you will find an olive tree (not the world's most northerly specimen — there's certainly one growing out-of-doors at the Cambridge University Botanic Garden, and possibly others farther up-country). The striking fern-like foliage of the honey locust, *Gleditsia triacanthos* 'Ruby Lace', makes a good foil for the extra-long flower spikes of *Buddleja davidii* 'Royal Red' and the silvery foliage of *B. d.* 'Lochinch', and for two sumptuously dark red roses ('Tuscany Superb' and 'Zigeunerknabe') and the altogether brighter — and massive — 'Cerise Bouquet'. The most fragrant rose in this small garden is *Rosa californica* 'Plena' — now, I believe, more correctly *R. nutkana* 'Plena' — curse the name-changing botanists! Whatever name it currently answers to, its bright little clear pink, semi-double flowers festooning long slender branches throughout July are a sure winner against even the costliest of couture perfumes and gentlemen's colognes. *Rosa* 'Moonlight', another semi-double, can also be

Top: The double-flowered *Geranium himalayense* 'Plenum' with *Rosa* 'Zigeunerknabe' in July
Above: *Stipa barbatus* in October sunlight

Top: A fallen stem of *Verbena bonariensis* and feathertop grass, *Pennisetum villosum*, August
Above: *Verbascum* 'Arctic Summer' with blue campanula, *C. lactiflora* 'Prichard's Variety', July

found in these borders, its aptly-named soft-white blooms glowing luminously after dusk over many weeks.

Earlier in the season there will be spikes of iris to admire. Irises seem to be favourites at Glyndebourne, their brief flowering period leaving behind clumps of sword-like leaves to contrast with flowers whose day has yet to come. 'Titan's Glory', 'Dusky Challenger', 'Croftway Lemon', 'Pink Lavender', 'Langport Flush' and 'Good and True' are some currently grown in the Urn Garden. And among the penstemons, those tough little perennials with small, foxglove-like flowers whose season extends well beyond the last opera to the arrival of October frosts, there are 'Garnet', 'Hidcote Pink', 'Primrose Thomas', 'Firebird' and 'Maurice Gibb'.

For matchless elegance, it is the salvias that steal the summer show in their inky shades of blue, mauve, and the kinds of reds the wardrobe department might seek when looking to dress the cardinals in a Verdi spectacular. All salvias have the hooded flower-shape typical of the genus, whether the familiar culinary sage or the plantsman's rare trophy carried away from the steamier parts of Mexico. Not all salvias are true perennials, however, plants which die down in winter only to reappear — usually as even larger specimens — the following spring. Some are annuals that need to be freshly raised from seed each year; others, like *Salvia sclarea* var. *turkestanica*, the biennial clary, have a two-year life cycle, producing massed spires of warm-pink-flushed white flowers in their second season. *Salvia × superba* will push its flower spikes more than three feet above ground level, so that its slender racemes of dark violet or purple flowers dance in the breeze above its companions.

A touch of the exotic has also crept into the Urn Garden over recent years — due, most likely, to Christopher Lloyd's influence. Here it is manifest in the yellow-flowering canna, or Indian shot plant, in the variety 'Richard Wallace' with bold, torch-like flowerheads that light up the garden on dull days. The cannas are not fully hardy, so Chris and the other gardeners must dig them up before hard frosts are expected, to spend their winter hibernation in a cold greenhouse, temporarily replanted in wooden wine crates — a commodity rarely in short supply at Glyndebourne.

THE UPPER POND

The Upper Pond, the 'top' pond in a string of five, is fed by the Glynde Bourne, one of many underground streams and springs that bubble to the surface from the chalk substrata of the Sussex Downs. From the Boathouse Lawn, close by the Urn Garden, you can still look through a mesh of willow branches to the same long stretch of water, flecked with water-lilies, that visitors to Glyndebourne's first opera season enjoyed in 1934. Winter gales have stripped the banks of some of their loftier trees, and the grass walk on the west side has been made wider in recent years, but none of the pond's great attraction for humans and wildlife alike has been diminished. Its circuitous path continues to provide opera-goers with their favourite pre-performance and interval walk.

Somewhere in the pond's depths lurks a massive concrete plug, buried now beneath tons of silt. In former days chains were fixed to the plug and a team of men and horses would pull it out to drain the pond for clearing the silt, and the accumulated mass of water-lily roots. The silt continues to build up, so a day will soon come when this mighty task will have to be attempted again — though machines will do the work of many men. The water-lilies, once much reduced in number by a water-borne disease, are now fit and healthy again — so much so that clumps have to be removed from time to time, to prevent the waters becoming completely choked with them. At present, the resident carp

Picnic by the Pond, 1965

glide freely. The extremely vigorous yellow flag iris (*Iris pseudacorus*) has successfully colonised one corner of the pond, its fleshy rhizomatous roots lodged happily in the silt and thick layer of clay which overlays the chalk.

The pond's grassy banks are mown once a year. In the spring, as the willow buds begin to swell and catkins dangle in the chill breeze, a few daffodils and early peony flowers enhance this tranquil scene. From the far end it's possible to glimpse the second pond in the string, and a third pond — once used by members of the Company for summer bathing — lies out of sight and out of bounds. Among the willows growing around the pond are a few specimen trees and shrubs, including silver birch, a walnut (one of several in the garden), bushes of winter-flowering viburnum, and euonymus (spindle) with its bright clusters of orange and red seed capsules in the autumn months.

THE NEW GARDENS

Construction of the new opera house in 1993/94 necessitated considerable re-modelling of adjacent areas. Three new gardens were made and the Kitchen Garden was 'moved' to a site between the Plashett Building and the Orchard.

THE KITCHEN GARDEN
AND ORCHARD

Lady Christie has a passion for tomatoes. Through the long summer months the Kitchen Garden is regimented with them — red tomatoes, orange tomatoes, yellow tomatoes (not to mention the still-green ones, ripening steadily for her future delectation). And the small greenhouse by the orchard will also be full of them. On a walk around the garden one August morning I was presented by Mary Christie with a perfectly ripe Victoria plum; she ate a tomato.

No country house is complete without its kitchen garden and here, on ground sloping between the Plashett Building and the orchard, is Glyndebourne's new vegetable plot. New it may be, but its function is traditional. In addition to the many rows of tomatoes, there are flowers for

Top: Bee hives in the orchard Above: The Kitchen Garden

cutting for the house, including fragrant sweet peas and roses. Potatoes, peas and beans, broccoli, chard, sweet corn and beetroot are grown, together with an assortment of lettuces and other salad leaves, and help feed the large numbers of house-guests made welcome throughout the summer. The wire netting in the surrounding beech hedge is designed to keep out rabbits.

Grass in the old apple orchard — where the pyramidal orchid also grows — is cut only in late summer, after the white mantle of cow parsley has flowered and seeded. The large aluminium-framed greenhouse is used for raising the many pelargoniums and other tender plants that stand out in pots in summer, and a small heated section provides winter quarters for those exotics that cannot take even one degree of frost.

THE MILDMAY GARDEN

The Mildmay Garden keeps alive the name of Glyndebourne's first Susanna, the Festival founder's wife, soprano Audrey Mildmay. The year before her death in 1953, when BBC radio broadcast from Glyndebourne one of its popular 'Down Your Way' programmes, hosted by Richard Dimbleby, Head Gardener Frank Harvey fittingly requested an aria from the last act (the 'garden act') of *The Marriage of Figaro*, sung by Audrey Mildmay. In 1965, Spike Hughes wrote that Audrey Mildmay's 'memorial is intangible because it

Cobaea scandens flowering in December in the Mildmay Garden

can be found only in the spirit of the Festival Opera and its faithful, un-relenting efforts to respect her famous dinner-table admonition.' (See page 15.) A more tangible memorial was subsequently effected in the form of a small garden (the Mildmay Dell), but this was sacrificed in the making of the Bourne Garden after the building work of recent years.

Now there is Mildmay Hall, built in 1993 to increase catering facilities to cope with the additional numbers of ticket-holders. Its barn-like design, with a massive hipped roof, is reminiscent of the original opera house, and its own relatively small garden — an enclosed courtyard with a lawn, a few apple trees and a long box-hedged mixed border backed by a high brick wall — recreates some of the atmosphere of the old walled garden which made way for the new theatre.

Although some of Mary Christie's favourite pink roses are accommodated here, it cannot be described as a rose garden in the true, old-fashioned sense. A vine and a passion flower grow on the high wall, as do a white solanum (like the one around the Green Room window), a jasmine, and the intriguing trumpet vine, *Cobaea scandens*, from Mexico. I've seen flowers on this climber in December, doubtless encouraged by the protection the wall affords against north and east winds.

One of the finest of all foliage plants grows in the border: *Melianthus major*, the honey bush, whose hollow stems carry a great wave of sea-green, softly-toothed leaves that might have been fashioned with pinking shears. Its curious brick-brown flower spikes may occur in late spring if winter weather spared the old growth. But if the plant falls victim to severe frost, its deep roots will preserve life underground until a new wave of foliage emerges the following season. Also from the southern hemisphere is the pittosporum, a handsome tree in all seasons, yet vulnerable to severely low temperatures or prolonged spells of cold winds.

THE FIGARO GARDEN

When Mary Keen imagined the Figaro Garden — whether in recognition of Glyndebourne's first opera, or as an idealised outdoor setting for its last act (the libretto asks only for pine trees and two arbours) — she had in mind something quite different in style from any other part of the existing garden, somewhere shady, yet ordered. Her search for a design took her back more than half a millennium, to the Middle Ages, when small monastic and manor house gardens alike were almost always enclosed, and divided simply into four quarters.

As the Figaro Garden's paths were also to serve as one of the pedestrian routes from car park to theatre, Mary Keen knew that surfaces needed to be free of mud or squelching grass. Bricks and paving were recycled from the old Walled Garden (where, approximately, sit the stage and backstage area of the new theatre), and a few of its treasured apple trees were transplanted to give a feeling of continuity. Unhappily, these did not survive the move and new ones were later substituted.

The garden could not be made until the contractors' earth-moving machines had finally lumbered away, leaving just a few nail-biting weeks before 1994's opening night in which to achieve a satisfactory, finished look. Sadly for designer, gardeners and plants alike, the ground vacated by the machines was so compacted that severe drainage problems quickly arose which could not be resolved in the fraction of time available. But although the original scheme did not survive in every detail, the gist and the mood are well conveyed, and before too long the designer's intentions will fully manifest themselves.

The keynotes are cool pink and pale blue, colours to invoke a certain calm, in deep contrast to the exuberant Bourne Garden next door, and to the theatre itself, rising like a cliff behind.

'Until the new apple trees have grown there is more variety in the planting,' says Mary Keen. Roses have been used for temporary effect until the apple trees are large enough to provide this garden with its intended measure of dappled shade. They are varieties with repeat- or continual-flowering habits — 'Felicia', 'Pearl Drift', 'Penelope', 'Old China Blush', 'Stanwell Perpetual', 'Comte de Chambord' and 'Bonica' — ensuring blooms for everyone, whatever

Top: Midsummer in the Figaro Garden Above: Agapanthus flowering in late July

day in the season they come. Most are grouped in threes of one kind to give bulk and plenty of flower (and perfume), and they are interwoven now with a legion of agapanthus, the 'Souvenir d'André Chaudron' catmint, and sky-blue *Campanula lactiflora*. The sundial at the centre of the Figaro Garden, commemorating the life of a young friend of the Christie family, was carved in 1993 by Geoffrey Aldred, and is a copy of an early sundial at Tapeley Park.

Overlooking the Figaro Garden is a new 'Green Room', for visitors rather than performers. The raised area of level lawn is gradually being enclosed by a wall of yew, with topiary shapes being trained to wire forms. A few years hence it will afford a sheltered spot for picnics, just a few strides from car park and theatre.

THE BOURNE GARDEN

Like its predecessor fifty years earlier, the new theatre opened its doors in 1994 to the strains of Mozart's *Figaro*. Writing in that year's festival programme Mary Keen said that 'the Bourne Garden is the surprise package. With show-off staircases cribbed from Covent Garden, and plants that are more Stravinsky than Rossini, it has a different spirit from the rest.' That 'spirit' is imparted by the fact that the land here dips steeply in places, distinguishing

Evergreen foliage of *Arum italicum* in the Bourne Garden

it from the rest of the garden's generally flat terrain, and by the decision to clothe it in jungly plants whose flowers take a subsidiary role to their foliage. This, perhaps, is 'where the wild things are'.

In high summer the Bourne Garden (taking its name from the stream, or bourne — the eponymous Glynde bourne — which runs underground to the string of ponds) is a dense forest of exotica. The sheer bulk of foliage encircling Henry Moore's sculpture of a reclining figure (which came to Glyndebourne through the Kahnweiler Bequest and is on loan from the Tate Gallery) is in no manner diminished by the new theatre towering above; rather, it forms a leafy buttress to the building, theatrical in itself, helping to soften hard architectural edges.

The prima donnas of this garden, introduced by Chris Hughes and his team, are the tall, pointed echiums (*Echium pininana*) with their fantastic spikes of soft pinky-blue flowers that have so successfully adapted to this foreign chalk. These prized echiums, native to the Canary Islands but brought to Glyndebourne originally from Tapeley Park, are classed as short-lived perennials, manifesting themselves here as triennials, which is to say that in the first year they stand as diminutive and somewhat fragile-looking seedlings; the following year they develop woody stems but grow only a few more inches; and in year three they then rise to ten, twelve, sometimes fifteen feet, carrying a profusion of hairy flowers right to the tip. Like giant bottle-brushes they oscillate in the summer wind. The whole plant dies after flowering, in the manner of the giant thistle in the White Border, but not before its myriad seeds have been released, many to find a safe toe-hold for another three-year cycle. As well as being short-lived, this echium is rated a half-hardy plant in the British Isles, one that runs the risk of succumbing to freezing temperatures. But so far enough have survived, against the odds, to secure its billing as Glyndebourne's new and improbable weed.

The banana trees are even more vulnerable to Sussex winters, and must be enclosed for several months in temporary timber-framed 'telephone kiosks' filled with bracken to keep them warm. The biblical papyrus, not hardy at all, is removed in October to the shelter of a frost-free greenhouse until the following spring. The tree ferns will survive temperatures as low as minus 10 degrees Centigrade, but as a precautionary gesture they are encased in polystyrene wraps.

Towering spires of *Echium pininana*

The Madeira geranium (*G. maderense*) is one of the world's largest cranesbills, a robust though short-lived perennial whose presence in this garden is again thanks to its ability to seed itself about. Progeny may be seen scattered all around the Bourne Garden, particularly in the shelter of hedges, where the dryer soil facilitates its survival.

Robust, too, are the canna lilies that stand like fleshy sentinels in fancy dress. *Canna indica* 'Purpurea' is brightly clad in orangey-red flowers, while *C. iridiflora*, from Peru, is as tall as a real guardsman by late summer, but flaunts unguardsman-like pink blooms above contrasting green leaves with a very thin purple margin. 'Wyoming', raised as long ago as 1906, has jumbo-sized dark leaves and orange flowers with apricot flashes. I see from nurserymen's catalogues that there are varieties named 'Meyerbeer' and 'Verdi': perhaps these too might be accommodated.

An admirable match for the cannas is *Dahlia imperialis*, from Guatemala and Columbia, although it is unlikely in this country to reach its potential height of thirty feet (unless, of course, the wildest threats about global warming come true). Leaves of the true tobacco, *Nicotiana tabacum*, from northern Argentina and Bolivia, can extend to fifteen inches in length, and their rose-

Tree fern, *Dicksonia antarctica*, and the midsummer flowers of *Geranium maderense*
in the Bourne Garden

The Bourne Garden. Top: Flower buds of *Acanthus mollis*
Above: Henry Moore statue of a reclining figure

flushed white flowers add powerfully to the fragrance of a warm summer's night. The wide palmate leaves of the castor oil plant (*Ricinus communis*) are shiny, reflecting flashes of light from dark corners. Red-flushed forms of this plant are raised at Glyndebourne from seed carefully selected by the gardeners each year.

Much of the Bourne Garden's vegetation is deciduous, so that with some plants cut to the ground or removed altogether in the winter, and others lying cosily under wraps, the scene from November through to April is in stark contrast to the lush jungle familiar to summer visitors.

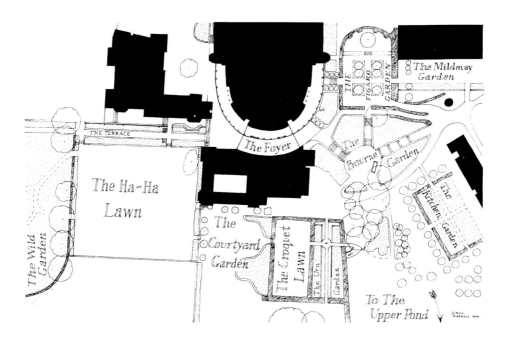

'These gardens', wrote Vita Sackville-West in 1952, are 'simply the inevitable prolongation of a man-made garden merging into the gently and tactfully assisted features of wood and water stretching away into what appears to be an illimitable distance.' Not so very much has changed.

Head Gardeners since the formation of Glyndebourne Festival Opera

Frank Harvey, 1934—1960

R. W. Hill, 1960—1966

G. F. Harris, 1967

Richard Grandis, 1968—1979

Terence Parker, 1980—1987

Christopher Hughes, 1988—

Notable Trees at Glyndebourne

Amelanchier canadensis (snowy mespilus), Wild Garden

Carpinus betulus (common hornbeam), Wild Garden

Catalpa bignonioides (Indian bean tree), Bourne Garden

Davidia involucrata (handkerchief tree), east side of Upper Pond

Fagus sylvatica 'Purpurea Pendula' (weeping purple beech), east side of Upper Pond

Gleditsia triacanthos (honey locust), Terrace

Juglans regia (common walnut), west side of Upper Pond

Liquidambar styraciflua (sweet gum), east side of Upper Pond

Liriodendron tulipifera (tulip tree), west side of Upper Pond

Morus nigra (black mulberry), Ha-ha Lawn

Platinus × *hispanica* (London plane), Turning Circle

Platinus orientalis (oriental plane), Boat House Lawn

Prunus avium 'Plena' (double gean), north side of Vegetable Garden

Quercus cerris (Turkey oak), Wild Garden

Quercus ilex (holm oak), several, particularly Wild Garden and one growing through the roof of Over Wallop restaurant

Salix alba 'Britzensis' (scarlet willow), several by Upper Pond

Salix alba var. *vitellina* (golden willow), several by Upper Pond

Tilia platyphyllos 'Rubra' (red-twigged lime), Wild Garden

Tilia cordata (small-leaved lime), front of Opera House

Birds seen in the garden at Glyndebourne

In addition to common garden birds (sparrows, chaffinches, robins and blue-tits), the following have also been recorded in the garden.

Barn Owl
Blackbird
Bullfinch
Buzzard
Canada Goose
Chiffchaff
Common Green Woodpecker
Coot
Cormorant
Crow
Cuckoo
Dove
Fieldfare
Goldfinch

Greater Spotted Woodpecker
Greenfinch
Greylag Goose
Heron
Herring Gull
House Martin
Jackdaw
Jay
Kingfisher
Lesser Spotted Woodpecker
Linnet
Little Owl
Long-tailed Tit
Magpie

Mallard
Mistle Thrush
Moorhen
Partridge
Pheasant
Song Thrush
Screech Owl
Sparrowhawk
Swallow
Swan
Tawny Owl
Woodcock
Wood Pigeon
Wren

If any keen-eyed bird-watching patrons are able to add to this list will they please advise the publisher so that subsequent editions of this book can be updated.

Bibliography

Binney, Marcus, and Runciman, Rosy, *Glyndebourne, Building a Vision*, London, Thames & Hudson, 1994

Blunt, Wilfrid, *John Christie*, London, Geoffrey Bles, 1980

Campbell, Susan, *Cottesbrooke*, London, Century, 1987

Ebert, Peter, *In This Theatre of Man's Life* (the biography of Carl Ebert, co-founder of Glyndebourne Festival Opera), Lewes, Sussex, The Book Guild, 1999

Hughes, Spike, *Glyndebourne: A History of the Festival Opera*, London, Methuen, 1965

Jolliffe, John, *Glyndebourne: An Operatic Miracle*, London, John Murray, 1999

Mabey, Richard, *Gilbert White*, London, Century Hutchinson, 1986

Keen, Mary, 'Work in Progress', article in 1994 Festival programme

Mawrey, Gillian, 'The Gardens of Glyndebourne', article in *Hortus* (No. 14, Summer 1990)

Sackville-West, Vita, 'The Gardens', article in 1952 Festival programme

Scott-James, Anne, and Lloyd, Christopher, *Glyndebourne: The Gardens* (with watercolours by Elizabeth Bury), Wendover, Bucks., The Peterhouse Press, 1983

Index

Page numbers in *italics* refer to illustrations

Picture Credits

Country Life: page 34; Simon Dorrell: (photographs and drawings) page viii, ix, 21, 24, 25, 38, 39, 45, 47, 48, 51, 56, 57 (bottom), 63, 65, 66 (bottom), 68, 73, 75 (bottom), 76; Glyndebourne Archive: page viii, 10, 12, 13, 14, 32; Guy Gravett: page ii, 17, 42, 54, 58 (bottom), 64; Mike Hoban: page i (top right, bottom left, bottom right), 19, 20, 23, 44; A. F. Kersting: page 35; London News Agency Photos Ltd: page 16; *The Times:* page 29; Topical Press Agency: page 58 (top); David Wheeler: page i (top left), v, 22, 26, 28, 30, 31, 33, 36, 37, 40, 41, 49, 52, 53, 57 (top), 60, 61, 66 (top), 67, 70, 71, 74, 75 (top).